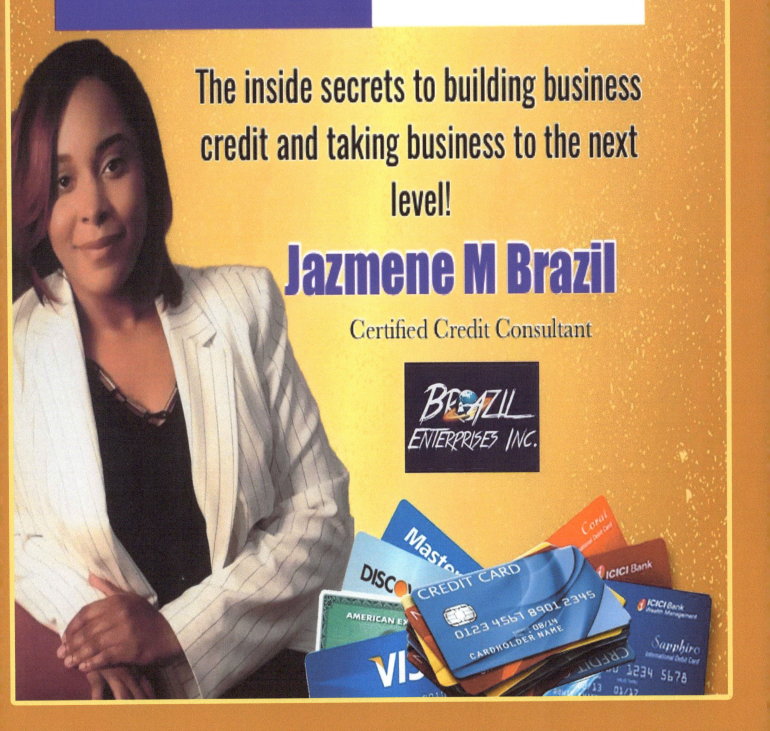

Copyright © 2020 by Jazmene Brazil. 814887

All rights reserved. No part of this book may be reproduced or transmitted in any form or by any means, electronic or mechanical, including photocopying, recording, or by any information storage and retrieval system, without permission in writing from the copyright owner.

To order additional copies of this book, contact:
Xlibris
1-888-795-4274
www.Xlibris.com
Orders@Xlibris.com

ISBN: 978-1-9845-8402-1 (sc)
ISBN: 978-1-9845-8403-8 (hc)
ISBN: 978-1-9845-8401-4 (e)

Print information available on the last page

Rev. date: 06/12/2020

PAYDEX Score	Payment Habit
100	Pays 30 days sooner than terms
90	Pays 20 days sooner than terms
80	Pays on due date
70	Pays 15 days beyond terms
60	Pays 22 days beyond terms
50	Pays 30 days beyond terms
40	Pays 60 days beyond terms
30	Pays 90 days beyond terms
20	Pays 120 days beyond terms
UN	Unavailable/no payment

DISCLAIMER

Information disclosed in this book is not to be duplicated, including useful business credit training by certified business credit instructors. The resource in question should be utilized as an educational resource to guide the everyday consumer on how to build business credit without the extent of needing to associate their consumer identification number. No information should be reproduced or duplicated. Any mention of information used from the text should be legally credited to its author Jazmene M. Brazil. Illegal distribution of this text will be legally taken, and legal ramifications may be enforced.

PREFACE

As a successful credit consultant, while working with business owners' personal credit, I was always eager to educate on the importance of the business credit world. However, I doubted myself many years before publishing it, in which the pages in my journal began to rip out during the 2020 pandemic. So here we are!

While working with consumers and realizing during this pandemic how small businesses were impacted financially. I knew then most consumers need to establish a capital for their businesses. It was like a message sent by the greatest of them all. Consumers and entrepreneurs NEED to be educated on business credit.

I'm bringing you ahead on a more simplified approach in which it will be easier to understand and it is straight forward. This will help you to grow your business or HELP someone else to grow their business.

Congratulations on a successful and wealthy business!

Jazmene M. Brazil

WHAT IS BUSINESS CREDIT?

Obtaining business credit is an important step for any business and helps you to: (1) maintain credit history in which it needs to be separated from personal credit and give you the experience for business benefits of having good business credit, and (2) demonstrate separation from the business and the owner.

WHY SEPARATE CREDIT HISTORIES?

By having a good business credit history separated from your personal credit, it prevents denials in the event one might have on the other. For Instance, if you have some financial issues on personal credit history and score or vice versa, that should not have an impact on one of the other credit profile. Be sure to separate the two from one another.

If you're not operating your business as a sole proprietorship or general partnership, you need to represent that the business is separated from the owner. The benefit of operating as corporations and limited liability companies (LLCs) is that you're protecting your personal liability.

Bonus Business Credit Tip: If you have an online business without a physical address, legally do not use a PO box for virtual business. Find a virtual office or rent a space and use that address.

IS IT TRUE THAT I CAN REALLY GET CREDIT FOR MY BUSINESS WITHOUT USING MY SOCIAL SECURITY NUMBER?

Yes, keep reading. It goes by no personal guarantee often abbreviated as *PG*.

WHAT IS DUN & BRADSTREET?

Dun & Bradstreet is the company that governs business credit profile for businesses. While the (known) personal credit bureaus are Equifax, Experian, and TransUnion for consumers' profile, the business credit bureaus and agencies are D&B, Experian, and Equifax. By obtaining your personally assigned nine-digit number, it puts you at an advantage because your business now will have a reported business score and profile. Take into consideration that the *higher* the score determines guaranteed acceptance and approval.

HOW DO I KNOW WHEN I CAN START BUILDING BUSINESS CREDIT?

- Proper licenses/bonds
- Registered legally in your state LLC or corp.
- Employer Identification Number
- Dun & Bradstreet number
- Business bank account
- Professional website
- Professional phone number
- Physical or virtual address
- Fax number
- Professional email (Hotmail, Gmail, Yahoo, etc., are not recommended)

Steps to Get Started

Step 1: Federal Employer Identification Number.

Visit www.irs.gov and obtain an Employer Identification Number. Complete the website application and after successfully completing the form you're assigned deration, if you have applied online previously before to obtain EIN, you will be required to call by phone to set up due to there being a maximum of times request can be made and received via the website.

Step 2: Ensure that your business entity is legally set up.

This step is *vital* to the growth of your business. Be mindful in order to build the business credit in the name of an entity, you must be a business recognized and filed by your state. If you need assistance with business structure, I recommend that you utilize www.legalzoom.com for your business support and setup. I suggest starting all business structures as a limited liability company (LLC) at the very minimum. If you need further assistance with how to structure or create, speak with a legal attorney over at Legal Zoom or consult with a local business attorney. With these contacts, you can obtain instructions on different levels of structures as well as assistance with setting up.

Bonus Tip: I recommend that you do the necessary research on your business name to ensure that it is not already in use prior to creating the name of your business entity.

You want to be sure that the business name is not infringing upon the rights of other companies. Visit www.uspto.gov/trademark and search under the "Trademark Search" to locate any existing companies that may have already secured a name. If you locate your business name there or anything similar, adjust your name.

Step 3: Online domains.

It's very critical that you secure your name and names you are associated with online. Knowing that online presence is ideal for building an online presence and audience. By taking these proper channels, this will prevent you from creating a name only to find out it's already in use. I suggest you visit www.godaddy.com and start your search there.

Step 4: Business bank account.

Business banking history is crucial to the development of business growth when you've incorporated your business (you will receive documentation by mail or electronically declaring your setup). However, once you have your Employer Identification Number, it's now time to make a trip to a local bank to open an account for business. My recommendation is that you open both accounts payables and accounts receivables to show that you mean BUSINESS. When building business credit, it's key that the plan being shown is a major corporation and expect to be treated as such.

Bonus Tip: Technically the date the account is opened is usually the date you are recognized as being in business. You want to open that account as quickly as possible.

Step 5: Professional business features.

Having professional business features are required! In order to be determined as a complete operating business structure, you should act as such! The very first step that should be taken is ensuring that you obtain a toll-free number, local number, and a fax number. There are several companies that can offer services like www.grasshopper.com, www.ringcental.com, etc., in which you can pay as little as $60 per month. All services are included in the disclosed price. Review websites to see which company works best for you. This all can be done and set up from the convenience of your cellular phone.

Having a professional website is also incredibly important! If you're on a tight budget and funds are low and can't afford professional assistance, build your website yourself. GoDaddy and Wix are great companies to have you create business websites. They will also allow you to set up a business with email and a virtual number.

Email addresses with @gmail.com, @hotmail.com, @yahoo.com are not permissible! Take into consideration that your email should always read your business name, for example name@yourbusinessname.com, org, etc.

It's also permissible to open a virtual address or create a business entity if you're an online business or working from your home. Companies like Regus are amazing and reasonable! You're able to purchase business address, have mail forwarded if need be, access to meet clients at a facility, use a conference/meeting room if needed for seminars, etc. Utilize Google or the Internet to search for Regus locations and any other virtual address companies in your area.

Step 6: Advertise and list your business online.

Advertising business online is incredibly important. If you're not advertising your business online, please do so ASAP to build your lead generation other than social media. It's all for free! You can list your business online at no additional cost. Before we proceed, yes, sales representatives may contact you to upgrade your packages but don't fall for the okeydoke! Here are sites you can register for FREE:

- Yellow Pages (www.yellowpages.com)
- Super Media (www.supermedia.com)
- ListYourself.net
- Local.com (www.local.com)
- Yelp (www.yelp.com)

Bonus Tip: By listing your business on these sites, this will attract additional revenue nationwide. Also do not use your personal home phone number. Lenders can determine your address is really a business-zoned address or indeed a home address.

Step 7: Setting up your business profiles.

- Experian business profile—<http://www.smartbusinessreports.com/>
- Equifax—1-866-519-4800
- Dun & Bradstreet—www.dnb.com

Bonus Business Credit Tip: Any business can obtain business capital and credit. The industry you're in does not matter.

BUSINESS CREDIT IS MADE UP OF THREE DIFFERENT TIERS

The tiers are:

- vendor/starter accounts

    These accounts are typically easier to receive approval and is the stepping stone to build your creditability. Business credit is no different from personal credit when it comes to building *creditability*. In order for other vendors to extend credit to you, you must build a solid and consistent payment history. You may be asked by some vendors to make payment upfront. Once all necessary factors to building credit are done, start to build vendor accounts which are also known as *Net 30*. I recommend you start with companies that offer such, such as Uline, Office Depot, and Quill.

- revolving store cards

    After you've built approximately five vendor accounts with solid payment history, UPGRADE. You're now eligible for the MAJOR STORE CARDS. Companies such as Walmart, Amazon, Target are just starters to name. I recommend having a minimum of ninety days of consistency payment history with vendor accounts first in order to apply for the store cards.

- cash credit

    This is to give you the ability to go straight to the source and actual lender. Take into consideration that this is where the MAJOR capital is derived from. Apply for Visa and Mastercard logo cards. These agencies also offer and extend cash.

Bonus Business Credit Tip: Majority of the businesses fail due to lack of cash reserve, funding, and lack of capital.

WHAT ARE THE ADVANTAGES OF HAVING BUSINESS CREDIT?

Having a good business credit can provide a number of advantages but not limited to:

- positioning your company to be offered more favorable credit terms
- having the option to have a more feasible interest rate or credit terms from lenders and banks
- reducing the number of times you will need to make prepayments for products or services purchased

How Do I Increase My Business Credit?

After establishing five or more vendor accounts, then move on to building store cards. I recommend having at least five cycles of payments before applying for store cards. As you make on-time payments with vendor accounts, BINGO, contact your lender to increase your credit limit. Take into consideration the higher the credit limits, the more CREDIT you will be approved for.

The key and secret to business credit—everything is based on making on-time payments.

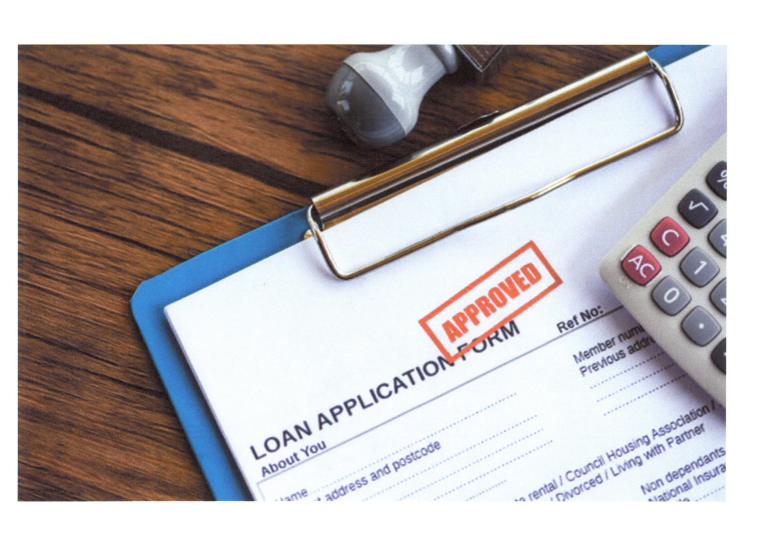

BUSINESS CREDIT INQUIRIES

Multiple credit inquiries are not looked upon as pleasant. If the required steps you are taking will be approved from start, denial shall not come into play. Please remember applying in phases is critical to avoid building excessive inquiries. While it's still up in the air for a lot of experts if inquiries actually affect chances of approval, I recommend you be cautious anyway! Your business credit speaks volumes, and it is your business profile.

Bonus Business Credit Tip: You cannot get business credit if you operate as a sole proprietorship.

CRITICAL HIGHLIGHTS

- Never be dishonest with company revenue. Some companies will require validation of income such as a copy of bank statements.
- Reframe from overdraft of banking account. Don't ruin your banking history.
- Ensure that you are not applying for too much business credit at once. A business credit profile is crucial, and you don't want to ruin your business credit profile.
- Be sure to apply strictly in your business's name solely.
- Do not place your personal social security number on your application.
- Use your EIN when applying for credit.
- Attach a copy of your Dun & Bradstreet number to your application or place it in the note section if listed on the application. When applying over the phone, you can also mention that you're established with Dun & Bradstreet.

HOW LONG WILL IT TAKE?

Once you have established everything, immediately start setting up vendor accounts. After five vendor accounts and three cycles of solid payment history, you're able to start store cards. After ten accounts, move on to the cash credit directly with Mastercard and Visa. All is determined by your drive. With determination and consistency, business credit can be earned in three to six months. Remember each lender has his/her set of requirements on what is required for approval.

BUSINESS CREDIT DIRECTORY

Business vendor accounts with requirements
No personal guarantee
Retail credit and requirements

Vendor accounts to start with:
Uline
FedEx
Quill
Reliable
Stamps.com
Staples

Business Credit Directory (cont.)

Accurate Office Supply (800) 621-5056
Requirements
PG: No
Paydex: No
Net 30, revolving account, 3 tradelines, and 1 bank trade. Call to have an application faxed to you.
It reports to D&B but does not report to Experian.

Best Buy (800) 811-7276
Requirements:
PG: No
Paydex: Yes, 65+

Chevron (888)243-8358
Requirements:
PG: Yes
Paydex: No
At least 2 years in business, DNB check revolving account, or Net 30. Apply online. It reports to D&B and Experian.

Conoco, Inc.
Requirements:
PG: Yes
Paydex: No
Net 30—full balance. Apply online located in 23 states. Ask for the locations. It reports to D&B and Experian.

€™s Electronics (714) 688-3000
Requirements:
PG: No
Paydex: No
Three trades, 1 bank trade, Net 30—full balance. Must submit financial and balance sheet before approval. It does not report to D&B or Experian.

Grainger.com
Requirements:
PG: No
Paydex: No
Net 30—full balance 1,000 min. credit limit, business license is needed along with 1 bank trade, and 2–3 other trades. It reports to D&B but not to Experian.

Home Depot (800) 685-6691
Requirements:
PG: No
Paydex: No (if 75 + Paydex, you will get an account as a young business) 2 years in business, revolving account, and Net 30. Apply online. It reports to D&B and Experian. It will issue for newer businesses if you have a Paydex score.

Kinko's (800) 488-3705
Requirements:
PG: No
Paydex: No
Revolving account and Net 30 are available. Apply online, will check D&B number, and verify your business address. It reports to D&B only when requested by D&B. It does not report to Experian.

Lowes (800) 244-6937
Requirements:
PG: No
Paydex: No, 75+
It will allow you to get one as a young business revolving account or Net 30, 3 years in business. It reports to D&B only.
Business Credit Directory (cont.)

Macys (800) 933-6229
Requirements:
PG: No
Paydex: No (75+ will allow you to get one as a young business)
Two years in business and some credit history. Call to have AN application faxed to you. It reports to D&B and Experian.

Nordstrom's: (800) 964-1800
Requirements:
PG: No
Paydex: No
Net 30—full balance, 3–4 trades, verify 2 (trades should be Net 30 accounts as well)
Call for application. It reports to D&B and Experian.

Office Depot (800) 729-7744
Requirements:
PG: No
Paydex: No
Revolving account, Net 30, must be incorporated. Print online and fax. It reports to D&B and Experian.

Office Max
Requirements:
PG: No
Paydex: No
Revolving and Net 30 available. Usually requires 2 years before issuing but have notices that if you get Net 30 then ask to change to revolving, this works. Required to have some credit history. Apply online. Payment has to be made after receipt of invoice. It reports to D&B and Experian.

Orchard Supply
Requirements:
PG: No
Paydex: No
Net 30, 3 trades with at least 3 months activity and 1 bank trade. Call to get an application. It does not report to D&B or Experian.

Phillips 66 Gas
Requirements:
PG: No
Paydex: Yes
Duns report pulled, 3 trades, 1 bank trade needed. It reports to D&B and does not report to Experian.

Sears (800) 917-7700
Requirements:
PG: No
Paydex: No (75+ will allow you to get one as a new business)
Two years in business, revolving account, Net 30. Call to get an application faxed to you. It reports to D&B and Experian.

Speedway Super America Fleet Gas Card (800) 643-1948
Requirements:
PG: No
Paydex: No
Net 30—full balance, at least 1 year in business

Staples (800) 669-5285
Requirements:
PG: No
Paydex: No
Revolving and Net 30 available. It reports to D&B and Experian.

Texaco (800) 839-2267
Requirements:
PG: No
Paydex: No
Need some credit history. Apply online. It reports to D&B and Experian.

Store cards to apply after establishing vendor accounts:

- Wal-Mart
- Target
- Amazon, Sam's Club, Shell, Keybank

IN NEED OF PROFESSIONAL BUSINESS CREDIT ASSISTANCE?

Building business credit is tedious and a little more complex than consumer credit. Jazmene has successfully been of assistance to many businesses, sharing information on business credit and on how to sustain business funding for their businesses. If you have a need for professional assistance, feel free to contact our office at 855-888-9222,

Monday to Friday, 8:00 a.m.–5:00 p.m. CST or feel free to schedule a business consultation via online www.brazilenterprises.org.

CPSIA information can be obtained
at www.ICGtesting.com
Printed in the USA
BVHW022301270620
582394BV00016B/16